Protect Our Planet

Disappearing Wildlife

Revised Edition

Angela Royston

capstone

© 2008, 2016 Heinemann Library
a imprint of Capstone Global Library, LLC

To contact Capstone Global Library, please
call 800-747-4992, or visit our website
www.mycapstone.com

Design: Joanna Hinton-Malivoire
Picture research: Melissa Allison, Fiona Orbell and Erica Martin
Production: Duncan Gilbert

Library of Congress Cataloging-in-Publication Data is available on the Library of Congress website.
ISBN: 978-1-4846-3591-9 (paperback)

Acknowledgements
The publishers would like to thank the following for permission to reproduce photographs: Alamy: Reynaldo Chaib Paganelli, 29; Getty Images: Berndt Fischer, 28, Minden Pictures, 17; Shutterstock: AuntSpray, 6, Brian Kinney, 21, David Steele, 26, dptro, 7, FloridaStock, cover, Gavin Baker Photography, 13, Gsubin pumsom, 14, GUDKOV ANDREY, 16, hristopher Wood, 20, James Michael Dorsey, 24, JaySi, 27, Krishna Utkarsh Pandit, 23, LMspencer, 5, Mary Nguyen NG, 12, ODM, 19, outdoorsman, 8, sergeisimonov, 10, SF photo, 11, Steven Fowler, 4, Volodymyr Goinyk, 15, Willyam Bradberry, 25

Every effort has been made to contact copyright holders of any material reproduced in this book. Any omissions will be rectified in subsequent printings if notice is given to the publishers.

Disclaimer
All Internet addresses (URLs) given in this book were valid at the time of going to press. However, due to the dynamic nature of the Internet, some addresses may have changed or ceased to exist since publication. While the author and the publishers regret any inconvenience this may cause readers, no responsibility for any such changes can be accepted by either the author or the publishers.

Contents

Some words are shown in bold, **like this**. You can find out what they mean by looking in the Glossary.

What Is Wildlife?

Wildlife is all the animals that live in the wild. It includes ocean animals and land animals. It does not include cows, dogs, and other animals that are kept by people.

Butterflies and other insects are types of wildlife.

There are many different types of animals.
Each type is called a **species**.

A leopard is a species of wild cat.

Endangered Species

Many types of animals that lived millions of years ago no longer exist. They are **extinct**. Dinosaurs are one type of animal that lived long ago. There are no dinosaurs alive today.

Mammoths are a type of elephant that no longer exists.

Today there are few mountain gorillas left in the wild.

Many **species** of animals are now in danger of becoming extinct. Gorillas are an **endangered** species. This means that there are so few wild gorillas they could die out.

What Is a Habitat?

A **habitat** is the place where an animal lives. Many animals can only live in a certain habitat. For example, polar bears live in the very cold lands in the **Arctic**. Camels live in hot, dry **deserts**.

Polar bears have thick fur and layers of fat to keep them warm.

You can see different types of habitats on this map of the world. The oceans are habitats too!

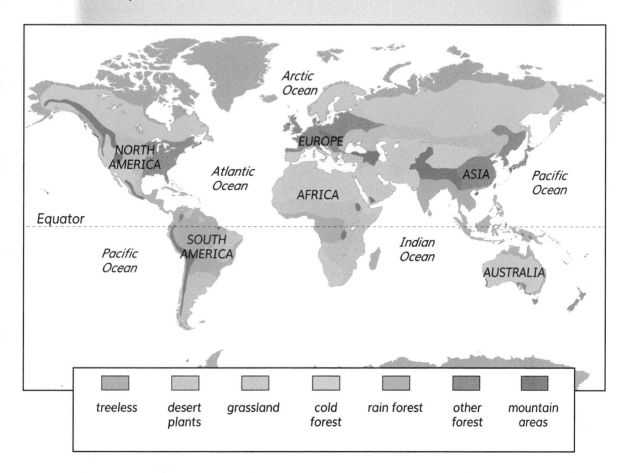

The world is divided into several main habitats. Each main habitat includes many smaller habitats. Even your local park is a habitat!

Changing Habitats

Habitats sometimes change. If a habitat changes very quickly, most of the animals that live there die. Habitats change for many reasons. Sometimes people damage or destroy habitats.

This wasteland is a habitat. The habitat will be destroyed when new offices are built.

Land at an airport is covered by concrete. Most wildlife cannot live here.

Building towns, airports, and roads destroys many natural habitats. The animals that live there die or move somewhere else. The new habitats have very little **wildlife**.

Farming

This large field is used to grow only one type of crop.

Farmers change natural **habitats**. Most natural habitats have a mixture of plants and many **species** of **wildlife**. Farmers plant just one type of **crop** in their fields. This means that fewer animals can live on that land.

Most farmers spray their crops to kill **pests** that harm the crop. The spray also kills butterflies, bees, and other wildlife that do not harm the crops. Very few animals live in these fields.

Planes are used to spray large areas of crops.

Disappearing Habitats

Some animals need lots of space to survive. Tigers hunt over a wide area to find enough food. As more land is used for farms and cities, tigers are in danger of becoming **extinct**.

Three **species** of tiger have recently become extinct.

Pandas need to spend at least 12 hours a day eating bamboo.

Pandas live in China and eat only bamboo shoots. Much of the land where bamboo used to grow has been cleared to make farmland. Pandas are now **endangered** because they cannot find enough bamboo to eat.

Cutting Down Forests

Rain forests are forests that grow in warm, wet places in the world. People are clearing large areas of rain forests. They cut down the trees to make farmland.

*Orangutans in Indonesia are **endangered**. The rain forest where they live is being destroyed.*

These frogs come from the rain forest.

Millions of different **species** live in rain forests. Many of these species are not found anywhere else. Scientists are afraid that some of these species will become **extinct**.

Changing Climates

The Earth is getting warmer. This is called **global warming**. Global warming is changing the **climate** in places around the world. This means that the usual weather in these places is changing. As the climate changes, the **habitats** change too.

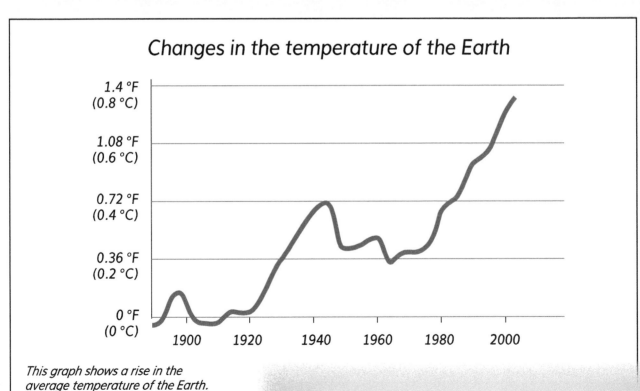

Changes in the temperature of the Earth

This graph shows a rise in the average temperature of the Earth.

Most of the rise in the temperature of the Earth has happened in the last few years.

*Only a few **species** can live in a desert.*

Many places get more rain than they used to, but many others get less rain. Less rain makes the ground dry up and the plants die. When **grasslands** dry up, they become **deserts**. Giraffes and other animals that live on the grassland have to leave.

19

Warmer Waters

The sea is warming up. This is making the ice in the **Arctic** melt. Polar bears creep across the ice to hunt for seals in the water. When the ice melts, they cannot reach the seals. If too much ice melts, polar bears may become **extinct**.

Some scientists think the polar bear could become extinct in 100 years.

coral

When a coral reef dies, the fish and other animals that live around it disappear.

Warmer seas are causing damage to **coral reefs**. Coral reefs are like ridges of rock. They are made of millions of tiny **shellfish**. If the water becomes too warm, the tiny shellfish die.

Hunting and Poaching

Some animals are hunted by people.
Elephants are hunted for their long ivory
tusks. The tusks are carved into ornaments
and jewelry.

Number of Asian elephants living in the wild

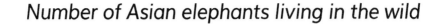

100
years
ago

today

 = 20,000

Poachers sell the horns of Black Rhinos for a lot of money.

Poachers are people who hunt animals illegally. Some poachers kill **endangered species**, such as Black Rhinos in Africa. The Black Rhinos are killed because their horns are used in some medicines.

Endangered Sea Animals

Some animals that live in the sea are also **endangered**. Some **species** of whales are endangered because they were hunted in the past. Many were hunted for their meat.

*This is a gray whale. Hunting nearly caused these whales to become **extinct**.*

dolphin

Some sea animals are killed by accident. In parts of the Pacific Ocean, dolphins and tuna often swim together. These dolphins can be killed by accident when they are caught in fishing nets with the tuna.

Protecting Wildlife

One way to protect **wildlife** is to make national parks. A national park is a large area of land where the **habitats** are protected. The wildlife is protected, too.

National parks are made where animals normally live. The land this elephant lives on has been made into a national park.

People who work for national parks try
to stop **poachers** from killing the animals.
Some people say that parts of the ocean
should also be made into national parks.

Charities That Protect Wildlife

Many **charities** work to protect **wildlife** and its **habitats**. They tell people about **endangered species**. They raise money to protect animals and the places they live.

This baby orangutan has no parents to teach it how to survive in the wild. It is being cared for by a charity.

You can become a member of charities that help protect wildlife.

You can help protect wildlife, too. Ask your librarian to help you learn more about wildlife in your area. Look up local charities that help protect wildlife. Everyone needs to work together to protect our wildlife.

Glossary

Arctic land and ocean around the North Pole where it is very cold all year round

charity group of people who collect money and spend it to make things better

climate kind of weather a place usually gets

coral reef ridge of hard coral made of the shells of tiny shellfish

crop plants grown by farmers to sell or use

desert area of dry land that gets very little rain

endangered in danger of becoming extinct

extinct when no members of a species exist any longer

global warming rise in temperature of the surface of the Earth, including the land, sea, and air

grassland land where the main plants are grasses. Grasslands are called prairies in North America and savannahs in Africa.

habitat place where certain kinds of plants grow and certain kinds of animals live

pest animal that eats farm crops

poacher person who hunts animals illegally

shellfish kind of animal that lives in the water and has a hard shell around its body

species *group of very similar plants or animals*

tusk *extra-long tooth that grows outside the mouth*

vet *doctor that heals animals*

wildlife *animals that live in nature without the help of people*

Find Out More

Books to Read

Gunzi, Christiane. *The Best Book of Endangered and Extinct Animals*. New York: Kingfisher, 2004.

Spilsbury, Louise and Richard. *Save the Giant Panda*. Boston: Heinemann Library, 2006.

Internet Sites

FactHound offers a safe, fun way to find internet sites related to this book.

Go to www.facthound.com

He'll fetch the best sites for you!

Index